T0334561

IRISH COFFEE

Cover Art: www.123rf.com

Author Photo: Ruth Hendricks
Cover and text design by Katherine Wintersteen
Titles and text set in Georgia

Printed on acid-free paper.

Coal Hill Review is an imprint of Autumn House Press, a nonprofit corporation with the mission of publishing and promoting poetry and other fine literature.

Coal Hill Review Staff
Editor-in-Chief: Michael Simms
Managing Editor: Adrienne Block
Assistant Editors: Alecia Dean, Caroline Tanski
Associate Editors: Giuliana Certo, Katherine Wintersteen
Intern: Nicole Bartley

PENNSYLVANIA COUNCIL ON THE ARTS   Autumn House Press receives state arts funding support through a grant from the Pennsylvania Council on the Arts, a state agency funded by the Commonwealth of Pennsylvania, and the National Endowment for the Arts, a federal agency.

ISBN: 978-1-932870-62-6

IRISH COFFEE

poems by **Jay Carson**

Coal Hill Review • Pittsburgh, Pennsylvania

Contents

In Saint Jude's Cemetery

Darkening in the evening half-light,
brothers and friends convince me
to enter a casket while alive,
to be buried for only a little while.

I will be safe, they pledge,
because of the dog at my feet
who will bark to warn them where
to come to dig me up fine.

But why must I half die anyway?
And if the dog chews through the sack to me?
I ask for time to think. They are
silver statues staring at the moon.

They are howling baby faces,
friezes in stone older than I will live.
As far as Uranus, they are as close
as the under-tongue pull at the start of retching.

Don't let us down again,
not like the last time.
We're counting on you.
The dog howls at the sack.

I think of running away
and wonder where I could go
to find a way from these, my people,
who know all my desires.

Bridge Cheese

My father had his Sunday cheeses,
difficult to pronounce and hard to hear,
for a ten-year-old, even one learning
bridge, the Roquefort and Camembert.

The deep steeped tea seemed all grown up,
and the piquant sandwiches squeezed
out silky teasing onion; tangy
potato salad oozed mayonnaise in seas.

But it was the cheese that was the knife
that yerked at my young guts.
They all smelled of rotten crumble,
the thought of mummies in rut.

Old was just the point my
young hand didn't comprehend,
my father tasting death
to finesse it to the end.

Sects

I am looking through the ornate complex
of iron bars that hold the altar
and, on its top, the big white lamb,
now in the sun, in St. Nicholas in Prague.
Christ must have appeared gentler to Jan Hus
than He did to the those who could not forgive
this first Protestant heresy. They roasted him.
His feast day is tomorrow.
This is his church.

Years ago, I was dating three women
at the same time. Yeah, they didn't
know either. I had to be fast on my feet
and keep them distracted, watching
the same chick flicks each wanted to see,
expensive dinners, away from each other's neighborhoods,
to say nothing of whatever they wanted sexually.

I'm into music and the arts now.
I go to concerts,
gallery openings, and plays,
and almost learned to read music once;
these church iron bars
remind me of the music sheets.

The sun is setting the lamb into the shade.
Beethoven just ended and now, Walther,
which is also the name of a pistol
once used to round up criminals.

Check

I stare at the final shreds
of my old checkbook;
little damage can still be done
to the fray of sleek
alligator hide that was
my brother's love,
belt-hard and smooth,
covering my loose spending.

As a child, he stole
all my dresser change
quickly spending it to nothing.

Later, he learned
to turn a buck
like kicking a bothersome leaf
in the cold wind.
Finding faith then in every
sad thing my father told him,
he tried to invest it back
in me: never to sell capital,
never to buy on margin,
never to co-sign
what you can't pay;
always to talk of money.

He never hit me
after I was twelve,
neither for the way

I mocked him nor how
I stole back
my time from him,
even as his checks
still floated me.

I take out from the billfold
a photograph of my brother, next to me,
formal, dark suits, serious faces,
very much in the bandit tradition.

Last Visit to My Aunt

I look down at my dying aunt,
the anthropology of my Celtic history, and see
my mother's, and my own skull staring back at me,
beautiful hair gone knotted to a question mark.

Is that paper mache mask telling
me some secret, in the mysterious unbroken
word stream that could be a keening for lost sisters,
a story from before I understood words?

A hundred runic prayers
run together for their eternity in the airy alleys
of her heaven, with its one incomprehensible God.
I add one more plea: please, get me out of here.

I can offer nothing now, and really
never could, except a hand to a stronger one
helping me perhaps across the street
or squeezing good bye on the train to camp.

I sneak my fingers away and watch
her hand rise, like a crippled duck,
now swimming somehow
smoothly into a glorious swan,
her wake finally empty of cygnets.

Irish Coffee

He sits with me at breakfast
and tells the horrifying story
about his brother's drinking, and stealing,
arrested with his saliva still staining
the rifle barrel. For we are Irish,

dreamy stallions with the bloodlines
that take us back to lost races,
to the knowledge that sooner or later
the world will break our hearts;
for we know the world of

dreams far better than is good.
We know its whiskey surge,
how it gathers to unleash the wizard
of our heart's tongue in a patriot game,
or loss on the water lapping at Innisfree.

I want to be horrified by his brother's excesses,
express sympathetic disgust, but
I am envious of his plans: take, shoot.
After my breakfast I lift coffee for a sip, already
planning for still another before it chills.

Peep Show: An Addict's Song

Well-hung neon wall tubes
embarrassed red, withered yellow,
call out, "Live Nude Models,"
as if we wouldn't look at a dead one.

In childhood, I hoped for kitchen sweetness,
expecting always, even alone,
the peach pie, despite these dirty hands'
surety: a filthy biscuit bite.

I have cooked up and spit out tales
of the sweetness of tasted peaches,
telling of the grab and circumference
of bouncing, cheesy rounds

bought, watched, and held down
below me, but that I could no more have
than the ineffable crumbling crust,
infinity of a loving baker's touch

that I search for in every shop.
In this salmon light I run out of time.
"Models changed five times daily"
to scour off my pressure-cooking stare.

Pittsburgh at Scorpio

November came down to Pittsburgh,
having laid waste the north trees, before
leaving them like mousy thrift shop sweaters,
shrinking on the stick bones
of old tree women. But first,
October came and set the city afire,
as if a maniac god had returned
the mills' burn everywhere.

Revolvers

The reservoir we walk around
is like glass today, reflecting
our lockstep reserve.
No dancing, only a few step
on the grass, little profanity,
no kissing. The repeated squeak
of sneakers on cement, until we are startled
by the cracking burst of pistols
from the firing range below,
reminding of all those shots thousands of miles away,
our faces repeating the sad blank stares
of the young, not starting, older, not finishing,
both with death and the smell of death.

Yet the buds never listen:
frozen out twice this year,
they are at it again.
And now the ducks start
their restless honking, repeating
a mirror of some lovely song
that is always a target.

A West Virginia Memory

Even in the early '60s, it was
like going back in time.
Not primordial, but when you
cut a hard mountain right, you were
lost in that God-swamp
of endless foliage. One of those turns,
they used to say
got Hank Williams at 29,
not far from here,
despite those great gospel songs.

And I wanted it, the absurd million-year
beauty of what wasn't blown up
by the coal owners, and those mine fields,
the too-many miners in the bars at 11:00 a.m.
because of a coal glut and their
own irascibility: *Two years now.*
Just wait for them to open,
I'll keep minin'. I wanted even
the feuds, polite, then deadly.
And the Fairmont ramp festival that Tom's
grandfather Babb didn't go to
because he got no personal invitation
for the first time in 30 years.
Wasn't sufficiently urged, he said.

And, stopping off at a contest or
the dances advertised on those small
waist-high portable billboards, that music

from hundreds of years ago to my gut today,
guitars, fiddles, banjos, even a man named Billy Banjo,
Archie Jones and his 12-string, all playing
our Appalachian heritage, the music of
the aging spine of our East.

West Virginia is the only state that still
legalizes snake handling, but also had
the only person who seemed to understand
the Vietnam War, my bartender, Sleepy:

late: honest-to-God outsized window
framing the glistening Monongahela River,
after my physical for the draft,
after the blended whiskey salesman left.
If they want to send them sons of bitches over here
and give me a gun, I'll shoot 'em.
But I'll be God damned if I'm going over there.

Flight

I watch the geese at the park nearby,
soaring in insolent unison to the faintest
heard song of the flock. They follow
wing to wing, mate for life: raise a family.
I watched my movers for evidence of missing silver,
bruised tables, broken family pictures,
stumbling out of joint
on the stairs countless times.

My friends are kind, "supportive," we say today,
but with eyes dreading
endless gloomy pizza evenings,
me sadly trashing an abandoned woman
for being herself.
How do the geese manage
to be always surrounded?
In the steel-encased apartment:
I can't call out.

I hear the stories; there must be
thousands of us, but no flock.
I long, perhaps for the children's wilderness camp
where the stubby and tall legs all fit
themselves in canoes, and the children search
the narrow and wide waters, singing
songs they make up of paddle and portage,
brave commitment in high harmony
rising, floating, in the tall Canada pines.

The Rat

I thought I had felt everything:
the Cartagena women teaching me
their scarf and sofa dance; the night
a hundred crows flew low above my house,
the hot breath of their wings in my hair; knees guiding
the sliding palomino, Killer, down the Rockies' stones.

But nothing touched me like the rat
scampering down my arm
from the garbage lid, skipping,
now thrown from my aorta to elbow
to flinging arm to the driveway edge,
down its length to a neighbor's rock hole.

I watched it go, slow
after the circus ride on too-pink me,
logy from eating through a heavy blue
plate of plastic trash can bottom, half
a bag of black peeled rind,
and now swaying chicken guts.

Ah, to love everything: from the fallen owl
to dead cat; to the moment between
the courses of the midnight repast,
when my poor Irish ancestors collapsed,
exhausted from their wake dance
and the next day's almost full burial.

The Hands of Mary Worth

Once when my son was breaking apart,
my wife held him briefly
and took his face into her hands
and smoothed it to its youthful faith.

Of all the absurd things
we ask women to do, soothing
is perhaps the most amazing,
drawing us toward them; assuring
us that death is an illusion, that we belong,
in the world, in their comforting hands.

The master artists
best capture that touch.

But if you are away from the galleries,
look at the daily comic pages
and see worthy Mary express, console
countless neighbors,
palm on breast, fingers
on throat, care radiating
out of the beautiful hands,
carrying the most overlooked gospel
of all the news.

Acknowledgements

The author wishes to thank the editors of the following publications in which these poems first appeared:

"Bridge Cheese"	*Distillery* (2003)
"Check"	*Xanadu* (2008)
"Flight"	*Stories About Time* (2008)
"In St. Jude's Cemetery"	*California Quarterly* (2005)
"Irish Coffee"	*Southern Indiana Review* (2005)
"Peep Show"	*Yalobusha Review* (2003)
"Revolvers"	*Summerset Review* (2011)
"Sects"	*Fourth River* (2011)
"The Rat"	*Louisville Review* (2006)
"The Rat"	*Pittsburgh City Paper* (2004)

A seventh generation Pittsburgher, Jay Carson teaches creative writing, literature, and rhetoric at Robert Morris University, where he is a University Professor and a faculty advisor to the student literary journal *Rune*. Jay regularly presents, reads, and publishes in local and national venues. More than 60 of his poems have appeared in national literary journals, magazines, and anthologies. He also co-edited with Judith Robinson *The Snow Falls Up*, a collection of Margaret Menamin's poetry. *The Cinnamon of Desire*, a full-length collection, is forthcoming from Main Street Rag in the fall of 2012. Jay considers his poetry Appalachian, Irish, accessible, and the derived spiritual survival of a raging, misspent youth—and just what you might need.

The Coal Hill Review
Chapbook Series

A Coal Hill Special Edition
Irish Coffee
Jay Carson

Winner of the 2011
Coal Hill Chapbook Prize
Bathhouse Betty
Matt Terhune

A Coal Hill Special Edition
Crossing Laurel Run
Maxwell King

Winner of the 2010
Coal Hill Chapbook Prize
Shelter
Gigi Marks

Winner of the 2009
Coal Hill Chapbook Prize
Shake It and It Snows
Gailmarie Pahmeier

Winner of the 2008
Coal Hill Chapbook Prize
The Ghetto Exorcist
James Tyner